HEAVENLY ASSIGNMENT

By
Pastor Innocent C. Ugo

Published by
Faunteewrites

Published by Faunteewrites Limited.

Copyright © Pastor Innocent C. Ugo 2025.

Chika I Ugo has asserted her right under the Copyright, Designs, and Patents Act 1988 to be identified as the author of this work.

This book is sold subject to the condition that it shall not, by way of trade or otherwise, be lent, resold, hired out, or otherwise circulated without the publisher's prior consent in any form of binding or cover other than that in which it is published and without a similar condition, including this condition, being imposed on the subsequent buyer.

Faunteewrites Limited,
Royal Arsenal Gatehouse, London, SE18 6AR.

Addresses for Faunteewrites limited can be found at:
www.fauntee.co.uk

A CIP catalogue record for this book is available from the British Library

ISBN:

978-1-913103-13-2—Paperback

978-1-913103-14-9—E-book

Without limiting the rights under copyrights reserved above, no part of this publication may be reproduced, stored in or introduced into a retrieval system, or transmitted, in any way or form, or by means (electronic or mechanical, photocopying, recording, or otherwise), without the prior written permission of both the copyright owner and the publisher.

TABLE OF CONTENTS

Introduction VII
Summary VIII

Chapter 1:
The Concept of Divine Purpose 1

Chapter 2:
Identifying Your Spiritual Gifts 7

Chapter 3:
The Power of Faith in Pursuing Your Assignment .. 11

Chapter 4:
Hearing God's Voice 15

Chapter 5:
Overcoming Fear and Doubt 19

Chapter 6:
The Role of Prayer in Discovering Your Assignment 25

Chapter 7:
Studying the Word for Direction 31

Chapter 8:
Why the Christian community is important 37

Chapter 9:
Recognising Divine Appointments 41

Chapter 10:
Developing Spiritual Discipline 45

Chapter 11:
Navigating Life's Challenges 49

Chapter 12:
The Connection Between Passion and Purpose 51

Chapter 13:
Stewardship of Your Talents 53

Chapter 14:
Walking in Obedience...................................57

Chapter 15:
Patience in the Process 61

Chapter 16:
Balancing Earthly Responsibilities and Heavenly Calling...65

Chapter 17:
 The Impact of Your Assignment on Others 69

Chapter 18:
Overcoming Setbacks and Failures.........................71

Chapter 19:
Continual Growth and Adaptation............................73

Chapter 20:
Living Your Divine Purpose Daily 77

References 81

HEAVENLY ASSIGNMENT

By
Pastor Innocent C. Ugo

INTRODUCTION

"Heavenly Assignment" by Pastor Innocent Ugo is a profound exploration of the divine purpose and calling that every individual possesses. Drawing from biblical teachings, Pastor Ugo emphasises each individual's unique assignment ordained by God, which aligns with the scripture found in Jeremiah 29:11: "For I know the plans I have for you," declares the Lord, "plans to prosper you and not to harm you, plans to give you hope and a future."

This book serves as both a guide and an encouragement for readers to discover their spiritual gifts and fulfil their divine destinies.

Pastor Ugo goes deeper to explore various themes such as faith, obedience, and the importance of understanding one's role within the body of Christ. He uses personal anecdotes, scriptural references, and practical applications to illustrate how individuals can navigate their spiritual journeys amidst life's challenges.

This book is a guide, encouraging you to seek God's guidance through prayer and reflection, echoing James 1:5: "If any of you lacks wisdom, let him ask of God, who gives generously to all without reproach, and it will be given to him."

SUMMARY

In **"Heavenly Assignment,"** Pastor Innocent Ugo delves into the profound concept of divine purpose, emphasising that every individual is uniquely created with a specific calling ordained by God. Drawing from biblical teachings, the book aligns its core message with Jeremiah 29:11, which reassures believers that God has plans for their lives—plans to prosper them and not to harm them. This foundational scripture guides the text, encouraging readers to seek out their unique assignments.

Pastor Ugo provides practical advice on how individuals can prepare themselves spiritually to fulfil their divine purposes. He emphasises the importance of prayer, studying the Word of God, and engaging in fellowship with other Christians as essential practices for spiritual growth and readiness. These elements are vital tools that empower believers to discern their callings and navigate their spiritual journeys effectively.

Moreover, "Heavenly Assignment" addresses common obstacles hindering individuals from pursuing their God-given assignments. Pastor Ugo identifies these hindrances and offers biblical solutions rooted in scriptures such as Philippians 4:13, which states that through Christ, believers can do all things. By providing insights and encouragement, the author aims to inspire readers to confidently overcome challenges and embrace their divine destinies.

This book is divided into several key sections that address different aspects of this journey:

1. **Understanding Your Purpose:** This section emphasises the significance of knowing one's purpose in life. It discusses how understanding our identity in Christ is foundational for fulfilling our heavenly assignments.

2. **The Role of Faith:** Here, Pastor Ugo highlights

the necessity of faith in executing God's plan. He references Hebrews 11:1: "Now faith is confidence in what we hope for and assurance about what we do not see," illustrating that faith acts as a catalyst for action.

3. **Obedience to God's Call:** He stresses that obedience is crucial for realising one's assignment. Drawing parallels with biblical figures who exemplified obedience to God despite challenges, encouraging you to trust in God's timing.

4. **Equipping Yourself Spiritually:** This section provides practical advice on how believers can prepare themselves spiritually through prayer, the study of the Word, and fellowship with other Christians.

5. **Overcoming Obstacles:** Pastor Ugo addresses common hindrances that may prevent individuals from pursuing their assignments; fear, doubt, and external pressures, and offers solutions grounded in scriptures like Philippians 4:13: "I can do all things through Christ who strengthens me."

6. **Living Out Your Assignment:** The final section focuses on taking actionable steps towards living out your assignment daily while remaining anchored in faith and community support.

Through these themes, "Heavenly Assignment" encourages you to discover your unique roles and actively engage in fulfilling them with passion and dedication. Understanding that when you align your personal goals with divine purposes, you can experience fulfilment and joy in your spiritual journey.

This book ultimately reminds us that everyone has a significant role within God's grand design, a message encapsulated beautifully in Ephesians 2:10: "For we are God's handiwork, created in Christ Jesus to do good works, which God prepared in advance for us to do."

LIVING YOUR DIVINE PURPOSE: A JOURNEY TO DISCOVERING YOUR HEAVENLY ASSIGNMENT

CHAPTER 1:

THE CONCEPT OF DIVINE PURPOSE

- Understanding God's plan for everyone
- Biblical foundation for personal calling
- Importance of aligning with God's will

Jeremiah 29:11

"For I know the plans I have for you," declares the Lord, "plans to prosper you and not to harm you, plans to give you hope and a future."

Figuring out what God has planned for each person

Divine purpose is understood through the idea that each person has a role in God's plan. This idea is backed by several Bible verses on how each person is created and called on purpose. For example, Jeremiah 29:11 says, "For I know the plans I have for you," which means the Lord knows they are beneficial and will not hurt you. They are plans to give you hope and a future. This verse emphasises God's specific plans for each person, suggesting that finding your holy purpose is essential to living a happy life.

The following biblical references offer more insight into the idea of God's purpose for each and everyone of us.

Ephesians 2:10

"For we are God's workmanship, made in Christ Jesus to do good things that God planned ahead of time for us to do." Meaning that each person is made with a purpose and is called to do things that align with God's will.

Knowing this essential part of God's plan for the world inspires Christians to look for their jobs through prayer, thought, and service to their community.

Philippians 2:13,

"For it is God who works in you to will and to act in order to fulfil his good purpose." Highlighting that God actively influences believers' desires and actions towards fulfilling His divine plan.

Romans 8:28

"And we know that in all things God works for the good of those who love him, who have been called according to his purpose." Affirming that everything in life can be woven together by God for the benefit of those who are aligned with His divine purpose.

A Biblical Basis for Personal Calling

The Bible is full of stories about people who God called to do certain things. In Exodus 3, God tells Moses from the burning bush that he is to take the Israelites out of Egypt. This is an example of a person who was called. This story shows that your personal calling often includes a direct experience with God and can cause big changes in your life. That's also shown in Isaiah 6:8, where the prophet hears God's voice asking, "Whom shall I send? And who will go for us?" Isaiah responds, "Here I am. Send me!" showing that he is ready to carry out God's plan. This text demonstrates how recognising your holy calling often requires preparedness and commitment.

Also, the New Testament expands on the lessons of personal calling. In Romans 12:4–8, Paul talks about the diverse gifts within the body of Christ, stressing that each member plays an important role in the functioning of the whole. He mentions various roles, such as prophesying, serving, teaching, and encouraging, illustrating that recognising one's talents is crucial for fulfilling one's divine purpose.

The following scriptures also illustrate how aligning with God's will is crucial to fulfilling your divine purpose:

Micah 6:8: "He has shown you, O mortal, what is good. And what does the Lord require of you? To act justly and to love mercy and to walk humbly with your God." Micah succinctly summarises what God requires of you as part of your calling.

Proverbs 31:8-9: "Speak up for those who cannot speak for themselves, for the rights of all who are destitute. Speak up and judge fairly; defend the rights of the poor and needy." This verse emphasises the call to advocate for justice and support the marginalised.

Why it's Important to Do What God Wants

To fulfil your spiritual purpose, you must follow God's will. Proverbs 3:5–6 advises, "Trust in the Lord with all your heart and do not lean on your own understanding; submit to him in all your ways, and he will make your paths straight." This verse stresses the importance of depending on God, rather than oneself, when seeking direction in life.

Furthermore, aligning with God's will typically involves prayer and Bible study to gain wisdom. James 1:5 assures Christians that if they lack wisdom, they should ask God, who gives generously to all without finding fault. This promise encourages believers that seeking God's guidance is both welcome and beneficial.

Realising your spiritual purpose involves reading the Bible and understanding God's unique plan for you. You can begin a meaningful journey towards fulfilling your divine assignment by exploring the biblical basis for personal calling and focusing on following God's will through trust and discernment practices such as prayer and Bible study.

1. **John 14:15:** "If you love me, you will keep my commands." This verse suggests a connection between loving God and obeying His commands. Genuine love for God is demonstrated through a willingness to do what He says.

2. **Romans 12:2** "Do not change to fit this world; instead, let the renewing of your mind change you so that you can find out what God wants, what is good, acceptable, and perfect." This verse encourages Christians to change by getting a new attitude, which will enable them to understand and follow God's will instead of giving in to worldly factors.

3. **5:17 of Ephesians** "So do not be stupid; know what the Lord wants." In this passage, Paul tells Christians to seek knowledge to know what God wants them to do. Figuring out what God wants and doing it is seen as a sign of spiritual growth.

4. **James 1:22** "Do not only listen to the word, deceiving yourselves; do what it says." This verse stresses doing things over just knowing things. It tells us not to get comfortable with our faith; doing what God wants is an important part of being a true follower.

5. **Matthew 7:21** "The only person who will get into the kingdom of heaven is the one who does the will of my Father who is in heaven." It's important to note that Jesus says vocal acknowledgement is not enough; doing God's will is what counts before Him.

6. **Colossians 3:23-24** "Do everything with all your heart, as if you were working for the Lord and not for people, because you know that the Lord will give you the inheritance as a reward." It says, "You serve the Lord Christ." These lines tell Christians that they should do everything with as much care as if they were serving God directly. From this point of view, every task has a feeling of meaning.

7. **Psalm 119:105** "Your word shines a light on my path and guides my steps." This verse shows how God's word helps us navigate life. Following His directions helps us make choices that are in accordance with His will.

8. **Proverbs 3:5-6** "Put your whole trust in the Lord; don't depend on what you think you know. Honour him in everything you do, and he will make your routes right.

   When you trust God instead of depending on your own insights, you can see clearly what your purpose and goal are, as He planned. 1. John 14:15: "You will follow my rules if you love me." This verse suggests that loving God and following His rules are linked. Truly loving God shows itself when we are ready to do what He says.

CHAPTER 2:

IDENTIFYING YOUR SPIRITUAL GIFTS

- Types of spiritual gifts
- Self-assessment techniques
- Recognising God's unique design in you

To fulfil your divine purpose, you need to understand and recognise your spiritual gifts. There are three main categories of spiritual gifts: ministry gifts, motivational gifts, and manifestation gifts. Each of these categories plays a specific role in a Christian's life and contributes to the functioning of the body of Christ as a whole.

Many kinds of spiritual gifts

- **Ministry Gifts:** Apostles, prophets, evangelists, pastors, and teachers are the "five-fold ministry" gifts described in Ephesians 4:11–12. These roles are crucial for building up the church and preparing the saints for service.

- **Motivational Gifts:** Romans 12:6–8 discusses motivational gifts, which are the inner drives that motivate individuals to serve God and others. These include prophecy, service, teaching, exhortation, giving, leadership, and compassion. Each gift addresses different needs within the community.

- **Manifestation Gifts:** 1 Corinthians 12:7–11 discusses these gifts, often understood as divine abilities bestowed by the Holy Spirit for specific purposes. Manifestation gifts can be further categorised into three groups: Revelation Gifts (such as the word of wisdom, the word of knowledge, and discernment of spirits). Power Gifts (such as faith, health, and wonders) Gifts of the Voice (like revelation, speaking in tongues, and interpreting tongues)

Techniques for Self-Evaluation

To find your spiritual skills, you can use the following self-assessment tools:

- **Spiritual Gift Assessments:** Different self-assessment tools can help you consider your experiences and natural inclinations towards certain groups or hobbies.

- **Prayer and Reflection:** Praying and reflecting provide an opportunity to ask God for guidance in understanding your unique design and calling.

- **Feedback from Others:** Your friends and church leaders can often offer valuable feedback on your skills and how they see you functioning in various roles.

- **Recognising God's unique design in You:** To recognise God's unique design for you, you need to understand how your spiritual gifts and personality traits interact. Psalm 139:14 proclaims that we are "fearfully and wonderfully made," highlighting God's intentional design for each individual. Because each person is unique, their spiritual gifts will manifest differently. Exploring and paying attention to your interests can also offer insights into your spiritual gifts. For example, if you are passionate about social justice issues, you may possess the gift of compassion or leadership. Similarly, if you enjoy teaching others about the Bible or life skills, you may have the spiritual gift of teaching.

Help from the Bible

According to the Bible, many people used their spiritual skills in the following ways:

- As a prophet, Moses led Israel out of Egypt (Exodus 3). He was a wonderful example of a leader.
- Paul as described in Romans 12 demonstrated enormous motivational gifts throughout his mission. Through extensive teaching and correspondence with early churches, he used his gift of encouraging others.

A Selection of Bible Verses on Spiritual Gifts

12:6-8 of Romans

This verse discusses different gifts, such as prophesying, serving, teaching, encouraging, giving, leading, and kindness. Every gift is given as a special way to help the body of Christ.

12:4-11 of 1 Corinthians

Paul discusses the different spiritual gifts that the Holy Spirit gives for the good of all people. Some of the gifts discussed are faith, healing, amazing powers, prophecy, speaking in tongues, gift of discerning spirits, and understanding tongues.

12:28 in 1 Corinthians

This verse provides more gifts, such as the ability to heal, help, lead, and speak different languages. It stresses the roles people play in church society.

4:11 Of Ephesians

This verse is more about jobs in the church than spiritual gifts themselves, but it does say that apostles, prophets, evangelists, pastors (shepherds), and teachers are important for equipping Christians.

4:10-11 in 1 Peter

People who believe in this verse are told to use their gifts to help others and share God's grace in all its forms.

2 Kings 2:4

This verse discusses how God revealed His word through signs, wonders, and miracles, as well as through the gifts of the Holy Spirit that He gave out according to His will.

These passages, when considered together, give you a complete understanding of the New Testament teaching on spiritual gifts. To sum up, figuring out your spiritual gifts isn't just about knowing what you can do; it's also about learning how those gifts fit into God's bigger plan for His church and the world.

CHAPTER 3:

THE POWER OF FAITH IN PURSUING YOUR ASSIGNMENT

- Definition of faith in a biblical context
- Examples of faith from scripture
- Cultivating unwavering belief in God's plan

Bible verses on **Faith**

1. **Matthew 21:22**—"And "whatever you ask in prayer, you will receive, if you have faith."
2. **Luke 1:37**—"For 'nothing will be impossible with God."
3. **2 Corinthians "5:7**—"For we walk by faith, not by sight."
4. **Romans 10:17** - "So faith comes from hearing, and hearing through the word of Christ."
5. **Hebrews 11:1** - "Now faith is the assurance of things hoped for, the conviction of things not seen."
6. **Hebrews 11:6** - "And without faith it is impossible to please him, for whoever would draw near to God must believe that he exists and that he rewards those who seek him."
7. **Ephesians 2:8-9** - "For by grace you have been saved through faith. And this is not your own doing; it is the gift of God, not a result of works, so that no one may boast."

8. **Proverbs 3:5-6** - "Trust in the Lord with all your heart, and do not lean on your own understanding. In all your ways, acknowledge him, and he will direct your paths."

9. **Mark 11:22-24** - "And Jesus answered them, 'Have faith in God. Truly, I say to you, whoever says to this mountain, 'Be taken up and thrown into the sea,' and does not doubt in his heart, but believes that what he says will come to pass, it will be done for him. Therefore, I tell you, whatever you ask in prayer, believe that you have received it, and it will be yours.'"

10. **James 1:5-8** - "If any of you lacks wisdom, let him ask God, who gives generously to all without reproach, and it will be given him. But let him ask in faith, with no doubting..."

11. **Philippians 4:13** - "I can do everything through him who strengthens me."

12. **James 2:19** - "You believe that God is one; you do well. Even the demons believe—and shudder!"

A biblical explanation of the word "faith."

When talking about the Bible, faith usually means believing in God and what He says. A basic meaning can be found in Hebrews 11:1: "Now faith is the assurance of things hoped for and the conviction of things not seen." This verse stresses that faith is trusting in God's promises, even though we may not yet see or fully comprehend their fulfilment. Faith is more than just agreeing with something; it's putting a lot of trust in God's character and His word.

The idea of being loyal and true to God is also part of faith. In the Old Testament, the Hebrew word for faith

(אֶרְנֶנָּה), emunah, meant something that was steady and trustworthy. In this kind of connection, Christians are asked to accept that God is good and in charge of their lives.

Bible verses that show faith

People who demonstrated extraordinary faith are talked about in great detail in the Bible:

- **Abraham**: Abraham's journey shows how to always believe in God's promises. He is often called the "father of faith." In Genesis 12:1-4, God tells Abraham that he will become a great nation if he leaves his home country and goes to a place he doesn't know. Abraham followed even though he was uncertain of what to do or expect. Evidence of Abraham's trust in God's plan.

- **Moses**: In Exodus 14:13–14, Moses told the Israelites not to be afraid, even though the Red Sea was in front of them and Pharaoh's army was behind them. He told them to stand strong and see how the Lord would save them. His faith helped them get through things that seemed impossible.

- **David**: David's fight with Goliath in 1 Samuel 17 shows how to have strong faith. Others were frozen with fear, but David spoke out and said, "The battle is the Lord's." He trusted that God would save them. His faith helped him win even though the odds were against him.

- **The Woman with the Issue of Blood:** This woman showed her faith in Mark 5:25–34 by thinking that if she could just touch Jesus' linen, she would be fixed. The things she did showed how strongly she believed that Jesus could heal her.

These examples highlight how faith is demonstrated through action. Even in uncertain or difficult situations, trusting God enables people to pursue their heavenly assignments.

Developing a firm faith in God's plan

To develop strong faith in God's plan for your life, it's essential to intentionally follow these practises:

Prayer and meditation: Talking to God every day through prayer makes our connection with Him stronger. Philippians 4:6-7 tells Christians not to worry but to give their wishes to God with thankfulness. This brings peace and confidence in God's plans.

Studying the Bible: Getting to know God's character and promises better through studying the Bible in depth. Romans 10:17 says, "Faith comes from hearing, and hearing through the word of God." This means that reading and hearing a lot of God's words can help you have more faith.

Community Support: Being around other Christians gives you strength and holds you accountable. In Hebrews 10:24–25, it says that Christians should not miss gatherings and should support each other on their spiritual paths.

Reflecting on the works of God: Remembering times when God was faithful in the past can help us believe that He still has plans for us. Psalm 77:11–12 tells Christians to think about what God has done and how amazing He is.

CHAPTER 4:

HEARING GOD'S VOICE

- Different ways God communicates
- Developing spiritual sensitivity
- Discerning God's voice from other influences

Bible Verses on Hearing God's Voice

1. **Jeremiah 33:3:** "Call me, and I will answer you and tell you great hidden things you have not known."
2. **Psalm 85:8:** "Let me hear what God the LORD will speak, for he will speak peace to his people and saints; but let them not turn back to folly."
3. **Psalm 119:105:** "Your word is a lamp to my feet and a light to my path."
4. **Mark 4:24:** "And he said to them, 'pay attention to what you hear: with the measure you use, it will be measured to you, and still more will be added to you.'"
5. **John 10:27:** "My sheep hear my voice; I know them, and they follow me."
6. **John 10:16:** "And I have other sheep that are not of this fold. I must bring them also, and they will listen to my voice. So, there will be one flock, one shepherd."
7. **John 14:26:** "But the Helper, the Holy Spirit, whom the Father will send in my name, he will teach you all things and bring to your remembrance all that I have said to you."

8. **Hebrews 4:12:** "For the word of God is living and active, sharper than any two-edged sword, piercing to the division of soul and of spirit, of joints and marrow, and discerning the thoughts and intentions of the heart."

9. **James 1:19:** "Know this, my beloved brothers: let every person be quick to hear, slow to speak, slow to anger."

10. **Revelation 3:20:** "Behold, I stand at the door and knock. If anyone hears my voice and opens the door, I will come into him and eat with him, and he with me."

Different ways God talks to us

God speaks to us in many ways, often according to each person's needs and situation. These verses offer insight into how God speaks, how to become more spiritually sensitive, and how to distinguish God's voice from other voices.

Scripture: The Bible is thought to be the primary way that God speaks to us. In Hebrews 4:12, it says, "For the word of God is alive and strong." It cuts through soul and spirit, joints and marrow, and is sharper than any double-edged sword. It judges the thoughts and attitudes of the heart.

This verse clarifies that the Bible is not just a collection of facts; it is also a live book that you can use to find your way.

Communication with God: You can talk to God directly through prayer. Paul tells us in Philippians 4:6-7 to pray and give thanks for our requests. He promises us peace in return: "Do not be worried about anything; instead, present your requests to God through prayer and petition, with thanksgiving."

Chapter 4: Hearing God's Voice

The Holy Spirit: The Holy Spirit is very important for leading us. "But when he comes, the Spirit of truth, he will lead you into all the truth," says John 16:13. This means that the Holy Spirit helps us understand what God is saying and helps us figure out what He wants.

Situations: God will sometimes use events or situations in our lives to show us what He wants us to do. Romans 8:28 tells us that "in all things God works for the good of those who love him." This means that our situations can show us how God is leading us.

Other believers: In the religious group, God often speaks through other believers. "As iron sharpens iron, so one person sharpens another," which means that other Christians can give you advice and knowledge.

Getting more spiritually aware

To hear God's words more clearly, you need to become more spiritually sensitive. This means becoming more aware of God's presence and paying attention to how He talks to us:

Practicing regular prayer and meditation: Praying every day helps us talk to God. "Be still, and know that I am God," says Psalm 46:10. This verse shows how important it is to be quiet to hear His words.

Studying the Bible: Reading and thinking about the Bible on a regular basis helps us understand who God is and how He talks to us (2 Timothy 3:16–17). This habit helps you become more familiar with religious concepts that help you make decisions.

Listening carefully: Making it a habit to listen instead of speaking during prayer can help you get closer to God (James 1:19). Paying attention makes it easier to receive divine direction.

Journaling your spiritual experiences: Writing down your prayers and thoughts in a book can help you see how God has spoken to you over time (Habakkuk 2:2). Writing down your thoughts may help you understand trends or signs from God better.

How to Tell God's Voice from Other Voices

It is essential for spiritual growth to distinguish God's voice from others through:

Testing against the scripture: Any word you think comes from God should match what the Bible says (Isaiah 8:20). It should not be taken seriously if it goes against the word of God or spreads lies.

Seeking confirmation: Often, getting confirmation through prayer or advice from spiritual leaders you trust can make things clearer (Proverbs 15:22). Multiple sources confirming a message can be a sign that it is the truth.

As a sign, inner peace: Colossians 3:15 tells us, "Let the peace of Christ rule in your hearts." If you feel peaceful after making a choice, it may mean that you are in line with God's will.

Recognising fruitfulness: Matthew 7:16 tells us that we will know real teachers by their fruits, which means that if they are from God, their results should be in line with His teachings.

Learning to recognise God's voice, becoming attuned to His guidance, and discerning it from other voices empowers us to pursue our divine purpose more effectively.

CHAPTER 5:

OVERCOMING FEAR AND DOUBT

- Common fears in pursuing divine purpose
- Biblical strategies for conquering fear
- Building confidence in God's promises

Bible Verses on Overcoming Fear and Doubt

Fear and doubt are common human experiences, but many Bible verses offer comfort and encouragement to overcome these feelings. These powerful scriptures offer guidance through moments of fear and uncertainty:

1. Isaiah 41:10 (NIV):

"So do not fear, for I am with you; do not be dismayed, for I am your God. I will strengthen you and help you; I will uphold you with my righteous right hand."

This verse reassures us that God is always present, providing strength and support in times of fear.

2. Psalm 23:4 (NIV):

"Even though I walk through the darkest valley, I will fear no evil, for you are with me; your rod and your staff, they comfort me."

Here, the psalmist expresses confidence in God's protection even in the most challenging circumstances.

3. John 14:27 (NIV):

"Peace I leave with you; my peace I give you. I do not

give to you as the world gives. Do not let your hearts be troubled and do not be afraid."

Jesus offers a profound peace that transcends worldly troubles, encouraging us to remain untroubled by fear.

4. Philippians 4:6-7 (NIV):

"Do not be anxious about anything, but in every situation, by prayer and petition, with thanksgiving, present your requests to God. And the peace of God, which transcends all understanding, will guard your hearts and your minds in Christ Jesus."

This passage emphasises the importance of prayer to combat anxiety and receive divine peace.

5. 2 Timothy 1:7 (NIV)

"For God has not given us a spirit of fear, but of power, love, and self-discipline."

This verse reminds us that God does not give us fear; instead, He empowers us with strength and love.

6. Psalm 46:1-3 (NIV):

"God is our refuge and strength, an ever-present help in trouble. Therefore we will not fear, though the earth gives way and the mountains fall into the heart of the sea."

This scripture encourages us to find refuge in God during tumultuous times.

7. Matthew 6:34 (NIV):

"Therefore, do not worry about tomorrow; tomorrow will worry about itself. Each day has enough trouble of its own."

Jesus teaches us to focus on today rather than being consumed by future uncertainties.

8. Romans 15:13 (NIV):

"May the God of hope fill you with all joy and peace as you trust in him so that you may overflow with hope by the power of the Holy Spirit."

This verse highlights how trusting in God can lead to joy and peace amidst doubt.

When we are trying to find and live out our unique purpose, we often encounter fears and doubts that hinder our progress. To overcome these fears, one must understand them, use Bible methods, and have faith in God's promises.

Thoughts on Common Fears in Pursuing Divine Purpose

Fear of Failure: We often worry that we won't be able to achieve our special purpose. This fear may stem from bad past events or a lack of faith in oneself.

Fear of Rejection: It can be scary to think about how other people will see your choices or you're calling. Because of this fear, people may be unable to take bold steps towards their goals.

Fear of the unknown: Going into unknown areas can make you nervous about what's ahead.

Fear of inadequacy: You may question your skills or credentials to do the things that are part of your spiritual purpose.

Biblical Ways to Get Over Your Fear

The Bible offers many ways to overcome fear, focusing on trusting in God's power and promises.

Prayer and Supplication: Philippians 4:6-7 tells us to pray and give our wishes to God. These steps will lead to a peace that is beyond our understanding.

Have faith in God's plan: In Jeremiah 29:11, the Lord

says, "For I know the plans I have for you—plans to prosper you and not to harm you, plans to give you hope and a future." This verse gives us hope that God has a good plan for our lives.

Scriptures that give us courage: Joshua 1:9 tells us to be brave and strong, and it also reminds us that God is with us all the time. This guarantee helps people who are afraid to follow their calling.

Community Support: Hebrews 10:24-25 talks about how important it is to get together with other Christians to help and strengthen each other on our faith paths.

What Makes Fear of God Different from Other Kinds of Fear

The idea of fearing God is very different from other kinds of fear. These verses will give you more insight:

Reverence for God's power and holiness is the foundation of the fear of the Lord (Proverbs 1:7), and it leads to wisdom and obedience. Fears like failure or rejection, on the other hand, often arise from a lack of trust or anxiety about the judgment of others, not from a true respect for God's power.

Psalm 111:10 talks about fear of God. "Being afraid of the Lord is the first step to being wise; people who practise it are smart." You are more likely to live a good life when you are afraid in this way.

However regarding fear of People (Matthew 10:28): Jesus says not to be afraid of people who can kill the body but not the soul. Rather, fear the One who can destroy both soul and body in hell. This emphasises the need to put divine power above human opinion of you.

Getting stronger faith in God's promises

Faith in God's promises overcomes doubt:

Verification from the Bible: "If God is for us, who can be against us?" Romans 8:31. This statement gives you courage in the face of fear.

Individual Testimonies: Thinking about times when you saw God keep His promises in real life helps you trust Him more. Isaiah 41:10 says, "Do not fear, for I am with you; do not be afraid, for I am your God." Keeping this verse close can help you fight doubt every day.

Acts of Faith: As you take small steps toward your divine purpose, relying on God's guidance, trust will develop over time.

To sum up, overcoming fear and doubt involves understanding common fears on this journey, using biblical principles through prayer and community support, discerning between different kinds of fear (particularly cultivating a reverent fear of God), and building unwavering confidence in His promises found in the Bible.

CHAPTER 6:

THE ROLE OF PRAYER IN DISCOVERING YOUR ASSIGNMENT

- Importance of consistent prayer
- Different types of prayer for guidance
- Creating a personal prayer strategy

The Role of Prayer in Discovering Your Assignment

Prayer plays a crucial role in the process of discovering our divine assignment. It serves as a means of communication with God, allowing us to seek guidance, clarity, and understanding regarding our purpose. Below are several Bible verses that highlight the significance of prayer in this journey:

1. James 1:5

"If you lack wisdom, let him ask of God, who gives to all liberally and without reproach, and it will be provided to him."

This verse emphasises the importance of seeking wisdom through prayer. When individuals feel uncertain about their assignment, they are encouraged to ask God for insight and direction.

2. Philippians 4:6-7

"Do not be anxious about anything, but in every situation, by prayer and petition, with thanksgiving, present your requests to God. And the peace of God, which transcends all understanding, will guard your hearts and your minds in Christ Jesus."

Here, Paul encourages believers to bring their concerns before God through prayer. This practice helps alleviate anxiety and opens the heart to receive God's peace and guidance regarding one's purpose.

3. Matthew 7:7-8

"Ask, and it will be given to you; seek, and you will find; knock, and it will be opened to you. For everyone who asks receives; he who seeks finds; and to him who knocks, it will be opened."

This passage underscores the promise that God responds to those who earnestly seek Him through prayer. It reassures believers that their efforts in seeking divine guidance will yield results.

4. Psalm 37:5

"Commit your way to the Lord; trust in Him, and He will do this."

This verse highlights committing one's plans or assignments to God through prayer. Trusting in His plan is essential for discovering one's true purpose.

5. Jeremiah 33:3

"Call me, and I will answer you and tell you great and unsearchable things you do not know."

God invites His people to call upon Him in prayer with the promise that He will reveal profound truths about their lives and assignments.

6. Romans 12:12

"Rejoice in hope; be patient in tribulation; be constant in prayer."

This verse encourages perseverance in prayer as a vital part of navigating challenges while seeking one's divine assignment.

What does it mean to pray?

In many religions, especially Christianity, prayer is a big part of everyday life. It's a way to talk to God, and it can include different kinds of talking, like praising, thanking, confessing, and asking. Prayer is a way to connect with God, ask for help, say what you need, and grow closer to God.

What Makes Intercession and Warfare Prayers Different

Prayers of Intercession: In this kind of prayer, you pray for other people. Stepping in to help someone else with their wants or problems is what it means. In James 5:16 (NIV), the Bible says, "The prayer of a righteous person is strong and effective." Intercessors often ask for people or groups to be healed, protected, or given direction.

Warfare Prayer: This type of prayer is about spiritual fights against bad forces and strongholds that stand in the way of God's will. Ephesians 6:12 (NIV) says, "For our struggle is not against flesh and blood, but against the rulers, against the authorities, against the powers of this dark world." This way of praying recognises that there is spiritual warfare. During warfare prayers, people often say statements of faith and tell evil spirits to stay away.

Why Consistent Prayer is Important:

Spiritual Development: Talking to God regularly helps us grow spiritually and strengthens our faith.

Guidance: We can get advice from God about our life choices and holy tasks if we pray daily.

Peace and Comfort: Philippians 4:6-7 (NIV) tells us not to worry but to pray and get what we want from God to feel at peace.

When you do not pray regularly, you might:

- not feel close to God.
- have trouble with worry or doubt without turning to God for help.
- not be able to hear God's words as clearly over time.

Different Kinds of Prayer to Get Direction

Prayers of thanksgiving: These are specific requests to God for things you want or need (Philippians 4:6).

Meditative prayer: is when you think quietly about the Bible or God's presence to get a better understanding (Psalm 46:10). This type of prayer focuses on being still before God so you can hear His words (John 10:27).

Prayer from the Bible: Reading and praying through Bible passages can help you align your thoughts with God's will (Isaiah 55:11).

How to Make a Plan for Your Prayer Life

1. **Set Aside Dedicated Time:** Pick times every day to pray without interruptions.
2. **Make a Prayer List:** Write down names or events that you want to pray for often.
3. **Incorporate the Bible:** If you want to get closer to God's word, use Bible verses as focus points in your prayers.
4. **Allow the Holy Spirit to lead you:** Be open to change when you pray, because God may lead you in ways you didn't expect.
5. **Think about your prayers:** Write down the answers to your prayers and the new ideas you have when you pray in a diary.

Chapter 6: The Role of Prayer in Discovering Your Assignment

These techniques are helpful in cultivating a deeper sense of meaning in connecting to your divine purpose.

CHAPTER 7:

STUDYING THE WORD FOR DIRECTION

- Importance of biblical literacy
- Techniques for effective Bible study
- Applying scriptural principles to life decisions

In this chapter, we will talk about the importance of knowing the Bible, the best ways to study it, and how to use biblical concepts to guide our choices. There will be appropriate Bible verses and examples to back up each part.

Bible Verses on Studying the Word for Direction

Studying the Word of God is essential for gaining direction and guidance in life. The Bible emphasises the importance of engaging with Scripture to understand God's will and to receive wisdom for decision-making. These key verses highlight this theme:

1. **Psalm 119:105:** "Your word is a lamp to my feet and a light to my path." This verse illustrates how God's Word provides clarity and guidance, illuminating the way forward in our lives.

2. **Romans 12:2:** "Do not be conformed to this world, but be transformed by the renewal of your mind, that by testing you may discern what is the will of God, what is good and acceptable and perfect." This passage encourages us to renew our minds through the Scripture, which helps us understand God's desires and make wise choices.

3. **Joshua 1:8:** "This Book of the Law shall not depart from your mouth, but you shall meditate on it day and night, so that you may be careful to do according to all that is written in it. For then you will make your way prosperous, and then you will have good success." Here, meditation on God's Word is linked directly to success and prosperity in following His guidance.

4. **2 Timothy 3:16-17:** "All Scripture is breathed out by God and profitable for teaching, for reproof, for correction, and for training in righteousness, that the man of God may be complete, equipped for every good work." This verse underscores the comprehensive nature of Scripture as a tool for equipping us in all aspects of life.

5. **Proverbs 2:6:** "For the Lord gives wisdom; from his mouth comes knowledge and understanding." This verse highlights that true wisdom comes from God's teachings found in the Scripture.

6. **Colossians 3:16:** "Let the word of Christ dwell in you richly, teaching and admonishing one another in all wisdom, singing psalms and hymns and spiritual songs, with thankfulness in your hearts to God." Engaging deeply with God's Word fosters community learning and personal growth in wisdom.

7. **Psalm 25:4-5:** "Make me to know your ways, O Lord; teach me your paths. Lead me in your truth and teach me, for you are the God of my salvation; for you I wait all day long." A plea for divine instruction emphasises reliance on God's guidance through His Word.

8. **Isaiah 40:31:** "But they who wait for the Lord shall renew their strength; they shall mount up with wings like eagles; they shall run and not be weary; they shall walk and not faint." While not explicitly about studying the Scripture, this verse reflects on waiting upon God's direction as part of spiritual growth.

9. **James 1:5:** "If any of you lacks wisdom, let him ask of God who gives generously to all without reproach, and it will be given him." This encourages us to seek wisdom from God through prayerful engagement with His Word.

10. **Hebrews 4:12:** "For the word of God is living and active, sharper than any two-edged sword..." This verse speaks to the power of God's Word as an active force that can guide our decisions effectively.

Why it is Important to Know the Bible

Biblical literacy means knowing and understanding what the Bible says, how it works, and what it means. It's important for several reasons:

Basis of Faith: The Bible is the most important book for Christians. Its lessons help us grow closer to God when we understand them. "So faith comes from hearing, and hearing through the word of Christ," Romans 10:17 says. This verse stresses the importance of reading and studying the Bible to grow in faith.

Help with Making Life Choices: The Bible gives advice and knowledge on many areas of life. Trust the Lord with all your heart and don't depend on your own knowledge, says Proverbs 3:5–6. Honour him in everything you do; he will make your routes right. This shows that knowing the Bible gives us the tools we need to ask God for help when making decisions.

Moral Framework: The lessons in the Bible give us a moral direction to enable us to decide what to do and how to act. "Your word is a lamp to my feet and a light to my path," says Psalm 119:105. This means that the Bible shows us how to act when we are faced with moral problems.

Tips for Studying the Bible More Effectively

There are several methods to help you understand and remember what you're studying in the Bible:

Contextual Reading: It is very important to understand the historical and cultural setting of bible verses. For example, understanding the lesson of the Good Samaritan story (Luke 10:25-37) about love and kindness across cultural borders is better when you know about the social norms of Jesus' time.

Meditation and reflection: Meditating on certain lines can help you understand them more deeply. Philippians 4:8 tells us to think about actual, honourable, just, pure, lovely, and praiseworthy things. This helps you to develop an attitude that is in line with God's values.

Group Study: Discussing or studying the Bible with others in a group can help you see it from different points of view. Acts 17:11 says that the Jews in Berea eagerly heard Paul's message, but they also studied the Bible every day to see if what he said was true. This shows how important it is to learn with others.

Use of Study Tools: Commentaries, concordances, and online tools can all help you understand complex texts. Bible Gateway and other websites like it offer many versions and learning tools that allow you to dig deeper.

Using Biblical Principles in Everyday Decision-Making

Once you know enough about the Bible through suitable study methods, it's essential to follow these rules:

Decision-Making Framework: Colossians 3:23-24 tells us to work hard as if we were working for the Lord and not for men. This principle can help you choose a job or behave appropriately at work by putting service above self-interest.

Conflict Resolution: Matthew 18:15–17 clearly outlines how to deal with disagreements in relationships. First, talk to the person who hurt you directly, then take things to the next level if necessary. This encourages healing based on biblical principles.

Life Goals Alignment: Jeremiah 29:11 tells us that God has plans for us, plans for our welfare and hope. This verse urges us to ensure that our personal goals align with God's purpose instead of focusing only on worldly success.

Incorporating these practices into your daily lives will enable you to better handle your spiritual journey while staying true to your faith.

CHAPTER 8:

WHY THE CHRISTIAN COMMUNITY IS IMPORTANT

- Role of the church in personal growth
- Finding mentors and accountability partners
- Serving others as part of your assignment

Being a part of a Christian group is very important for spiritual and personal growth. Getting involved with a church or social group provides a safe place to explore your faith, grow your skills, and find your divine mission.

How the Church Provides Spiritual Growth

For its members, the church is an important place to grow in their religion and in their daily lives. It offers many things that are necessary for spiritual growth, like training, prayer, and community. Hebrews 10:24-25 (NIV) says, "Let us think about how we can encourage each other to love and good deeds. Let us not stop getting together, as some people tend to do, but let us encourage each other; and all the more as you see the Day coming." This verse stresses how important community is for building support and holding people accountable.

Churches also often have programmes like Bible studies, prayer groups, and classes that help people understand the Bible better and find ways to use it in their daily lives. Taking part in these church events, you will grow spiritually and make friends with others members.

Finding Mentors and Accountability Partners

For personal growth, having a mentor in the church is very important. Having a guide can help you on your spiritual journeys by giving you advice, support, and direction. In Titus 2:3-5 (NIV), it says that older women should teach younger women how to live by God's rules. This shows how mentoring works in the Bible, where more experienced Christians help teach younger Christians.

Having accountability partners is also a great way to stay spiritually disciplined. "As iron sharpens iron, so one person sharpens another," says Proverbs 27:17 (NIV). This shows how holding each other accountable and encouraging each other can help us grow spiritually.

Helping Others is Part of Your Assignment.

One important part of living out your spiritual purpose is helping other people. The Bible is full of stories about people who gave their lives to help others:

Jesus Christ: Jesus is the best model of someone who serves others. He says in Mark 10:45 (NIV), "Even the Son of Man did not come to be served, but to serve." Service to others shaped his life. He healed the sick, fed the hungry, and taught those who needed it.

Moses: Moses led his people out of slavery in Egypt as a service to them. In spite of his initial reluctance (Exodus 3:11–12), he agreed to serve God by leading and guiding his people.

Dorcas (Tabitha): In Acts 9:36–42 (NIV), Dorcas is called a follower who is known for her kindness and good deeds. Her life was an example of service because she did real things that helped her society.

Paul: Apostle Paul spent his whole life sharing the Gospel and starting churches all over the Roman Empire, even though he was persecuted for it (2 Corinthians 11:23–28). In many of his writings, he tells Christians to love each other and help each other.

These few examples show that helping others goes beyond just an action but that a person is committed to doing what God has planned for their life.

In conclusion, being a part of a Christian community enables you to grow as a person through shared experiences, guidance, accountability partnerships, and group service projects that are in line with your holy purpose.

CHAPTER 9:

RECOGNISING DIVINE APPOINTMENTS

- Understanding God's timing
- Identifying opportunities aligned with your purpose
- Responding to unexpected doors opening

Recognising Divine Appointments

Recognising divine events means being aware of times in your life that are planned by a higher power and often lead to important meetings or chances. There are many lines in the Bible that talk about how important it is to be aware of these divine acts and see God's hand at work in our lives. Here are a few important Bible verses that support the idea of noticing when God makes plans for us.

1. Proverbs 16:9: "The heart of man plans his way, but the Lord establishes his steps."

This verse makes it clear that even though we may have our own ideas, God eventually decides what we should do. To recognise divine visits, we need to be aware that God's plan may change our plans, bringing us to surprising but important meetings.

2. In Isaiah 30:21: "And when you turn to the left or right, you will hear a word behind you that says, 'This is the way, walk in it.'"

This reading shows how God leads us by speaking to us and telling us what to do. Being in touch with this advice can help us figure out when we need to make a choice or when we are at a crossroads.

3. Acts 8:26-40: (Philip and the Eunuch from Ethiopia) In this story, an angel of the Lord tells Philip to go south to the road that goes from Jerusalem to Gaza. There, he meets an Ethiopian gentleman reading the Bible. He can describe what it means, which leads the eunuch to be baptised. This story is a great example of how divine arrangements can change the lives of everyone concerned.

4. In Romans 8:28: "And we know that all things work together for the good of those who love God and are called according to his plan."

This verse tells us that everything that happens in our lives is part of God's plan. Recognising divine arrangements means having faith that even things that seem odd can be part of God's bigger plan.

5. 2 Corinthians 2:10: "For we are his work, made in Christ Jesus for good works that God planned ahead of time so that we would do them."

This is where Paul talks about how God made us for specific jobs and good deeds. We are more likely to take advantage of these chances when they see them as divine appointments.

6. Colossians 4:5: "Be wise with strangers and make the most of your time."

This verse tells us to be aware and deliberate in how we connect with others. Being present and aware during everyday interactions is often necessary to see heavenly meetings.

7. Matthew 10:16: "Look, I'm sending you out like sheep among wolves. Be as smart as snakes and as pure as doves."

Jesus tells those who follow Him to be wise and aware of their surroundings as they face problems. This ability

Chapter 9: Recognising Divine Appointments

to discern is very important for figuring out when God might be working through people or situations.

To sum up, noticing heavenly meetings requires being spiritually aware and willing to let God guide you through your daily life. The above texts show how the Bible supports this idea by showing that God is in charge of our lives and telling us to keep our eyes on where He leads.

CHAPTER 10:

DEVELOPING SPIRITUAL DISCIPLINE

- Creating habits that nurture spiritual growth
- Fasting as a tool for clarity
- Balancing spiritual practices with daily life

Cultivating Habits that Help Mental Growth

If you want to develop mental discipline, regular habits are a must. The Bible stresses how important it is to do things on a daily basis that help you grow spiritually.

1. Timothy 4:7-8 (NIV) says, "Do not believe in myths and old wives' tales that are not based on truth. Instead, train yourself to be godly." Because getting in shape is helpful in some ways, but being holy is always useful and holds hope for both this life and the next.

This chapter shows how important it is to train yourself in godliness, just like you would train your body. It says that we should form habits that are good for their spiritual health, just like sports professionals do to stay fit.

2. Hebrews 12:1 (NIV) says, "Because we are surrounded by so many witnesses, let us get rid of everything that stands in our way and all the sin that is so easy to catch." And let's keep going as we follow the path that has been set out for us.

This verse tells Christians to develop habits that help them stay focused on their spiritual path, eliminate things that confuse them, and stay true to their faith.

Fasting for Spiritual Clarity

In the Bible, fasting is an important practice that people do to get clarity and closer to God. This is a basic verse about fasting:

Matthew 6:16-18 (NIV): "when you fast, don't look sad like liars do. They change the way their faces look to show that they are fasting. They really did get their full prize, I promise you. But when you fast, wash your face and rub your head with oil so that no one else can see that you are fasting but your Father, who sees everything. He will repay you because He knows what you do in secret."

This chapter tells us how to fast in a humble and sincere way, instead of trying to get attention from other people. Fasting can help you get closer to God and understand what He wants you to do better.

Isaiah 58:6, says that God wanted people to fast in this way so that the chains of evil would be broken and all yokes would be broken.

This verse shows that real fasting is more than just not eating; it also includes acts that show God's kindness and justice. People who believe in God should do acts of service and love while they fast.

How to balance spiritual activities with everyday life

Finding a balance between spiritual practices and daily duties can be hard, but it's necessary for growth in all areas. The following are guidelines from the Bible:

Colossians 3:23-24 (NIV) says, "Do whatever you do with all your heart, as if you were working for the Lord and not for people." This is because you know that you will receive a gift from the Lord. You are following the Lord Jesus Christ.

This text reminds us that every job can be an act of worship and encourages us to include our spiritual lives in all parts of our daily lives, even at work.

Phil 4:6-7 (NIV) says, "Do not worry about anything; instead, bring your requests to God in every situation through prayer and petition, with thanksgiving." And the peace of God, which is greater than all understanding, will keep your minds and hearts safe in Christ Jesus.

Here, Paul stresses the importance of prayer as a way to stay calm when life gets tough. This combination of relying on God through prayer and daily work shows how spiritual practices can fit into everyday life.

To sum up, spiritual training is

- Spiritual training is part of making habits (1 Timothy 4:7-8).

- Fasting is a way to get clarity (Matthew 6:16–18).

- To keep your spiritual life in balance, you must put your faith to work (Colossians 3:23–24).

CHAPTER 11: NAVIGATING LIFE'S CHALLENGES

- Viewing obstacles through a spiritual lens
- Learning from biblical characters who faced adversity
- Finding strength in trials

Spiritual Approaches to Challenges

When you're going through hard times, looking at them through a spiritual lens can help you understand them better and feel better. People with this perspective are more likely to see problems not just as failures but also as chances to learn and grow. In the Bible, James 1:2-4 says, "When you face trials of many kinds, consider it pure joy, my brothers and sisters, because you know that the testing of your faith makes you strong." Let patience do its job so that you can be fully grown and complete, with nothing missing. This verse stresses that trials can help us grow as people and as spiritual adults.

Romans 8:28 also comforts us: "And we know that God works all things for the good of those who love him and have been called according to his purpose." In other words, it means that even when things look bad, God has a plan that can turn problems into gifts.

Lessons From Challenges of Biblical Figures

The Bible is full of stories of people who went through tough times and came out better and more faithful. Job is a well-known example. Job went through a lot of pain—losing his family, having health problems, and losing all of his money, but he stayed true to his faith. He famously said in Job 1:21, "The Lord gave and the Lord took away; may the name of the Lord be praised."

His story shows how strong people can be when they are going through terrible things, and it shows how important it is to keep your faith when things get hard.

Another example is Joseph, whose brothers sold into slavery and then put him in jail without a good reason. Even though things were hard, Joseph stayed honest and had faith in God. He eventually became king of Egypt and saved many people from starvation (Genesis 50:20). His story shows how sticking with something, even when things get hard, can help you reach your goals.

Building Strength Through Trials

When things get tough, people often need to lean on their faith and their group for strength. "I can do all things through him who gives me strength," Philippians 4:13 says. This verse emphasises the idea that Christians have the strength to get through hard times because God is with them.

Also, Hebrews 12:1-2 tells us to "run with perseverance the race that was set out for us," looking to Jesus as an example of how to be patient. This verse tells us that our problems are not unique and that we can find strength in Christ's own trials.

In real life, praying or meditating with literature can help us work through our problems and find comfort. Support from the community is also very important; sharing problems with others can make us lighter (Galatians 6:2).

To sum up, dealing with life's problems through a spiritual view means seeing problems as chances to grow and getting ideas from bible characters like Job and Joseph. We can become more resilient in the face of hardship by finding strength in our faith and the support of our community.

CHAPTER 12:

THE CONNECTION BETWEEN PASSION AND PURPOSE

- Identifying God-given passions
- Aligning personal interests with divine assignment
- Pursuing purpose with enthusiasm

Finding your God-given interests

To find your God-given interests, you have to look inside yourself and pray about what makes you happy and fulfilled. Psalm 37:4 says, "Delight yourself in the Lord, and he will give you what your heart desires." This verse makes the point that people can see their real interests more clearly when they align their hearts with God's will.

For instance, someone may have a strong desire to help others, which could show up as a strong interest in social work or community service. This wish could be seen as a sign of how much God loves people. Talents, like the ability to teach or create art, can also show where someone's interests lie. In Exodus 35:30-35, the Spirit of God fills Bezalel to make beautiful designs for the Tabernacle. This shows that God can inspire people with certain skills.

Putting Personal Goals in line with God's Mission

To align your personal goals with God's callings, you need to know your unique gifts and how they fit into your bigger plan. Romans 12:6-8 says that each of us has unique skills that come from God's kindness. We should use these gifts to help other people. For example, if someone loves music, they might think about how they can use that love to help their church group or share words of hope through worship.

Take King David's life as an example. He was not only a leader but also a singer and songwriter. His psalms show how deeply he felt and how much faith he had. They also show how his personal hobbies fit with his spiritual calling as a leader and worshipper (1 Samuel 16:23). You can better understand your divine tasks by figuring out how your hobbies connect with opportunities to help others or praise God.

Going After a Goal with Excitement

To enthusiastically pursue meaning, one must actively take part in activities that satisfy both personal desires and divine callings. Colossians 3:23 says that we should "work heartily, as for the Lord and not for men." This verse emphasises how important it is to be dedicated to your goal. People often find more joy and effect in their work when they do it with a passion that comes from their faith, whether they are in ministry, business, or creative pursuits.

Take Mother Teresa as an example. She spent her whole life helping the poorest people in Calcutta. Her unshakeable dedication to her goal and never-ending efforts to help those in need showed how much she cared. "Not everyone can do great things," she said one time. We can show a lot of love in small ways, though. This shows how enthusiastically following your purpose can make big changes in your life and the lives of others.

In short, finding your God-given passions means praying about what makes you happy and then focussing on that. Aligning your personal interests with your divine assignments means understanding how your unique gifts serve God's purposes, and pursuing your purpose with passion will lead to actions that make a difference and show your faith.

CHAPTER 13:

STEWARDSHIP OF YOUR TALENTS

- Understanding the parable of the talents
- Developing and using your abilities for God's glory
- The responsibility of maximizing your potential

Matthew 25:14-30 tells the story of the gifts, which is a key source for understanding stewardship in a biblical context. In this story, before going on a trip, the master gives each of his workers different amounts of money, which are called "talents." When he gets back, he looks at how each worker handled the things he gave them to do. The first two servants put their skills to work and double their amounts. The third servant, however, hides his talent out of fear. The boss praises the first two workers for their hard work and scolds the third for not doing anything.

Several important ideas are shown in this story:

God Gives Us Skills: Just like the boss gave his workers skills, God gives each person their own skills and chances (Romans 12:6-8). Some of these are spiritual tools, skills, and gifts that we are supposed to grow and use. We have a responsibility to use our gifts. It's clear that we should use our skills instead of hiding them. This fits with James 1:17, which says that every good gift comes from above. This means that our skills are gifts from God that are meant to be used for good.

Accountability: The story ends with a review of each servant's work, which reminds us that we are responsible for how we use our skills (2 Corinthians 5:10). Being responsible for our actions pushes us to reach our full potential instead of wasting it.

Building up your skills and using them for God's glory

To improve our skills and use them well for God's glory, we need to do a few things:

Self-Evaluation: It's important to know what your skills and flaws are. Ephesians 2:10 tells us that God planned ahead of time for us to do good things. To figure out what those works might be, you have to think about yourself and pray.

Education and Training: It's important to spend time learning new things and getting better at the ones you already have (Proverbs 22:29). Improving your skills, whether through official schooling or personal growth, gives you the tools you need to do your job better.

Service Opportunities: Looking for ways to help others puts your skills to use in the real world (Galatians 5:13). Doing volunteer work or church events can give you chances to show off your skills.

Collaboration: Your effect can be greater when you work with others (Ecclesiastes 4:9–10). By working together as a group or team, you can use your different skills to make things better.

Continuous Growth: Being a good steward is not a one-time thing but a process that goes on all the time (Philippians 3:12-14). Reevaluating your goals and looking for new tasks on a regular basis will help you keep getting better.

The Duty of Making the Most of Your Potential

The Scripture makes it clear that maximising ability is both a gift and a duty:

Faithfulness Over Success: Being good caretakers should be the main goal, not just being successful (Luke 16:10). Being faithful means always trying to get better, even if you don't see results right away.

Effects on Others: Using your skills in a good way has a positive effect on those around you (Matthew 5:16). When you do good things and let your light shine, it honours God and encourages others to do the same.

Building a memory: Our memory is affected by how we use our skills (Proverbs 13:22). Investing in the next generation by teaching or training them will make sure that our skills keep giving long after we are gone.

Eternal viewpoint: Keeping an eternal viewpoint helps us decide how to spend our time and money most wisely (Colossians 3:23–24). Knowing that our work will have long-term effects drives us to do our best in everything we do.

To sum up, being a good steward of one's talents means recognising divine gifts, actively developing them through education and service, working with others, prioritising loyalty over success, making a positive difference in people's lives, leaving a legacy, and keeping an eternal perspective on our efforts.

CHAPTER 14:
WALKING IN OBEDIENCE

- The importance of obedience in fulfilling your assignment
- Overcoming personal desires that conflict with God's will
- The blessings that come from faithful obedience

Why Obedience is Important for Getting Your Work Done

Many religions, especially Christianity, stress the importance of obeying your leaders. A lot of people see it as a way to achieve their divine mission or purpose. Several passages in the Bible stress how important it is to follow the rules. For example, Jesus says in John 14:15, "If you love me, follow my rules." This verse makes the point that following God's rules is a sign of real love for Him.

Additionally, loyalty is more than just following the rules; it shows that we trust and are loyal to God. God tells His people in Jeremiah 7:23, "Obey me, and I will be your God, and you will be my people." This promise from the covenant makes it clear that obeying God is necessary to feel his presence and follow his lead.

Biblical characters give clear examples of this concept. Think about how Abraham was ready to leave his home country when God told him to (Genesis 12:1-4). His obedience helped build a great country and brought him gifts that went beyond his own life. Similarly, Moses's submission to God's command to lead the Israelites out of Egypt (Exodus 3) shows how doing what God says can have big effects on the world.

Getting Past Wants That Are at Odds With God's Will

One of the hardest things for Christians is balancing their own wants with God's will. Galatians 5:17 says, "For the flesh desires what is contrary to the Spirit." This is something the Bible recognises. Because of this tension, you have to choose to put your spiritual needs ahead of your material ones.

Jesus prayed, "Not my will, but yours be done" in the Garden of Gethsemane to show how hard this was for Him. This moment shows how human desire and divine purpose are at odds with each other. Jesus' willingness to do what God wanted led to the saving of all people.

When we have different wants, we are told to pray and study the Bible to get God's direction. It says in Proverbs 3:5-6 to "trust the Lord with all your heart and not rely on your own understanding." If you do this, he will make your paths right. People who believe this text are reassured that giving up their own goals can help them achieve their divine purpose.

The Good Things That Happen When You Follow Directions

As guaranteed throughout the Bible, faithful loyalty brings many benefits. People who follow God's rules will be blessed, as stated in Deuteronomy 28:1-2: "If you fully obey the Lord your God...all these blessings will come on you." These blessings cover many areas of life, such as mental wealth, good health, and peace in relationships.

James 1:25 also says that when we carefully study the perfect rule that sets us free and then stick to it, not forgetting what we have learnt but doing it, we will be blessed in what we do. As this verse says again, actively obeying God not only brings heavenly happiness but also real benefits in everyday life.

Chapter 14: Walking in Obedience

There are many cases from real life of people who have received great blessings by obeying. For example, preachers who have dedicated their lives to helping others often say they are deeply happy and fulfilled, even when they are going through hard times. This shows that real blessings come from matching your life with God's plans.

To sum up, walking in obedience means realising how important it is to complete sacred tasks, resolving personal conflicts with God's will through prayerful submission and receiving many gifts as a result of following His instructions faithfully.

CHAPTER 15:
PATIENCE IN THE PROCESS

- Understanding God's timeline vs. personal expectations
- Lessons from biblical figures who waited on God
- Developing perseverance in pursuing your purpose

Knowing God's Timeline vs. Your Own Expectations

In life, people often have to deal with the difference between their own schedules and what they think God's timeline is. Tension like this can make people angry and irritable, especially when their own needs aren't met quickly. There are many cases in the Bible that show how important it is to wait on God's time.

The story of Abraham and Sarah is a good example of this. In Genesis 12:1-4, God tells Abraham that he will have a lot of children and raise a big family. But Sarah doesn't give birth to Isaac until Genesis 21:1-2, which is a long time after they had planned to have children. This wait shows us that God's promises may take a while to come true, but they always do, because He has a perfect plan.

Genesis. 37–50 tells us about the life of Joseph, which is another powerful example. Joseph becomes powerful in Egypt after his brothers sell him as a slave and he endures years of suffering. Through his trip from jail to palace, we can see how God's plans often take a long time and involve difficult situations. In Genesis 50:20, Joseph tells his brothers, "You meant to hurt me, but God meant it for good." This makes him think about this. In this, it's shown that even though we don't understand what's going on or why, God has a bigger plan.

Lessons From People in The Bible Who Waited on God

There are many examples in the Bible of people who showed patience and faith while they were waiting. Another important person whose life shows this concept is Moses. Moses meets God at the burning bush (Exodus 3), forty years after leaving Egypt and living in Midian (Exodus 2:15-25). He had to spend a long time getting ready, but it was important for him to play his part as the leader who would free Israel from slavery.

In the same way, David didn't actually take the throne for many years after being crowned king (1 Samuel 16; 2 Samuel 5). He went through a lot of trouble during this time, including being persecuted by King Saul. David often had trouble waiting, but he also had faith in God's plan (Psalm 27:14 says, "Wait for the Lord; be strong and take heart, and wait for the Lord").

These stories are strong reminders that waiting is not an idle thing to do; it takes faith and trust in God's control. Each bible character had their own problems, but in the end, they all learnt that waiting was key to their spiritual growth and to God keeping his promises.

Developing the Willpower to Keep Going After Your Goal

When trying to reach your goal, you need to be persistent, especially when delays or problems come up. The New Testament tells us to stay strong even when things get hard. James 1:2-4 says, "When you face trials of different kinds, think of it as pure joy, because you know that the testing of your faith makes you strong." This text makes the point that trials are chances to grow.

Throughout his mission, the Apostle Paul showed resilience by being jailed, beaten, and shipwrecked (2 Corinthians 11:24–27). Even though things were hard, he was determined to spread the Gospel. This shows us today that we should stay focused on our holy calling no matter what is going on around us.

Also, Hebrews 12:1 tells us to "run with perseverance the race that has been set out for us." This picture suggests working hard towards your goal while believing that God will lead you along the way.

Finally, to understand the difference between God's timetable and our own, we need faith-based patience. Waiting can lead to deep spiritual growth and purpose fulfilment if you are persistent. Biblical figures like Abraham, Joseph, Moses, David, and Paul demonstrated this.

CHAPTER 16:

BALANCING EARTHLY RESPONSIBILITIES AND HEAVENLY CALLING

- Integrating your assignment into daily life
- Managing time and resources effectively
- Finding purpose in everyday tasks

Putting Your Assignment into Your Daily Life

In the Bible, there are many examples of people who showed how to carry out God's plans in their daily lives. Nehemiah, who was told to rebuild the walls of Jerusalem, is a good example of this. Even though he had to deal with resistance and problems, Nehemiah did a good job of managing his duties by putting prayer and action first. He put people in order, gave them jobs to do, and kept his eye on his goal while also taking care of the needs of his community (Nehemiah 4:6). His ability to balance his spiritual calling with his everyday duties is a great example of how to live out your calling in real life.

Bible verse: "So we rebuilt the wall until it was only half as high as it was before. The people worked hard." It says in Nehemiah 4:6

Let's look at Martha from the New Testament instead. Jesus told her, while she was busy with housework, how important it was to feed her spirit rather than just getting things done (Luke 10:38–42). This shows that our duties on earth are important, but they shouldn't get in the way of our calling divine assignment.

Bible Verse: "Martha, Martha," the Lord said, "you are worried and upset about many things that you don't need to be worried or upset about." (NIV) Luke 10:41–42

How to Effectively Manage Time and Resources

Matthew 25:14–30 tells the story of the gifts, which shows how to effectively manage time and resources. In this story, before going on a trip, the master gives each of his workers different amounts of money, which represent their skills. When the master comes back, the servants who used their skills wisely are honoured. This tells us about care, which means being good with the things God has given us so we can do our jobs.

Bible verse: The master told him, "Well done, good and faithful servant!" Some things you have done right; now I will put many things in your hands. (NIV) Matthew 25:21

Proverbs 21:5 also talks about planning and hard work when it comes to handling resources: "The plans of the diligent lead surely to abundance, but everyone who is hasty comes only to poverty." This verse tells us to think carefully and plan ahead in everything we do, whether it's spiritual or not.

How to Find Meaning in Everyday Tasks

Ruth's life shows how to find meaning in the things you do every day. As a widow working as a gleaner in Boaz's fields (Ruth 2), Ruth showed loyalty and dedication, even though things were hard for her. Not only did her hard work save her, but it also played a key part in God's plan for Israel because she was related to King David.

Bible verse: Ruth responded, "Don't tell me to leave you or turn away from you," as it says in the Bible. I will follow you wherever you go and stay where you stay. (NIV, Ruth 1:16)

Chapter 16: Balancing Earthly Responsibilities and Heavenly Calling

To find meaning in our work, we are told in Colossians 3:23–24 to do it as if we were serving the Lord instead of people: "Whatever you do, work at it with all your heart; it is the Lord Christ you are serving." From this point of view, everyday jobs become acts of worship.

In short, bible characters like Nehemiah show how to fit projects into daily life. Parables like "The Talents" teach how to manage people well, and characters like Ruth show how to find meaning in everyday tasks. Each case shows that it is possible to balance responsibilities on earth with callings from heaven if you are faithful and deliberate.

CHAPTER 17:

THE IMPACT OF YOUR ASSIGNMENT ON OTHERS

- Understanding the ripple effect of fulfilling your purpose
- Inspiring others through your obedience
- Building a legacy of faith

Realising How Achieving Your Mission will Affect Other People

Several bible characters give powerful examples of the idea of a "ripple effect" in achieving one's goals. For example, Moses's response to God's call not only freed the Israelites from slavery in Egypt, but it also set off a chain of events that would shape the whole country of Israel. Many people were moved by his leadership and loyalty, including Joshua, who later led the Israelites into the Promised Land. This shows how dedicated to their spiritual calling one person can be and how that can affect generations.

Exodus 3:10-12 (NIV) is an important verse because it says that God tells Moses, "Now go." I want you to go to Pharaoh and get my people, the Israelites, out of Egypt. When Moses finally agreed to go on this journey, it changed everything for his people and their future.

Motivating Others by Following Through

The story of Esther is another strong one. When she went up to King Xerxes, she was brave and ready to speak up for her people. This shows how individual obedience can lead to group action. "And who knows but that you have come to your royal position for such a time as this?" Esther famously asked in Esther 4:14 (NIV), showing that she knew what she was supposed to do. Her efforts not only kept her people from being wiped out, but they also gave them strength to stick to their faith.

Esther's story shows how respect and selflessness can bring a whole community together to work towards a shared goal. This reinforces the idea that what we do can motivate others to reach their own goals.

Leaving a faith-filled

People like Abraham left behind lasting examples of how being true can make a difference. Abraham was an important person in Judaism, Christianity, and Islam because he always believed what God said would happen. Genesis 12:1-3 (NIV) tells us that he was ready to leave his home country and do what God told him to do: "The Lord had said to Abram, 'Go from your country, your people, and your father's household to the land I will show you.'"

Abraham's children carry on his tradition, and he continues to show us how important it is to have faith and follow through. His life makes us think about what kind of impact we are leaving behind when we do things.

The mission of Paul in the New Testament also shows how one person's hard work can affect many people. Millions of people around the world are still moved by his letters. In Philippians 3:13–14 (NIV), Paul talks about pushing on towards his goal, which can inspire people who want to grow spiritually.

Putting these examples together shows that doing your holy duty has effects beyond just you. It has ripple effects that encourage others to be faithful and inspire them to follow their own goals.

CHAPTER 18:

OVERCOMING SETBACKS AND FAILURES

- Dealing with disappointment and perceived failures
- Learning from mistakes and growing stronger
- Maintaining faith through difficult seasons

How to Deal with Failure and Disappointment

Many people in the Bible went through big losses and setbacks, but they were able to get through them by having faith and being strong. One well-known example is Moses, who at first couldn't get Pharaoh to free the Israelites from slavery. After a few plagues, Pharaoh's stubbornness might have made Moses want to give up. He kept believing in God's plan, though, and eventually led the Israelites out of Egypt (Exodus 3–14). This shows us that failures can be part of a bigger plan from God.

Peter is another example. Three times while Jesus was being tried, Peter rejected Him (Luke 22:54–56). Peter felt very bad about failing at this, and it made him feel hopeless. But after Jesus rose from the dead, Peter was forgiven (John 21:15–19) and became one of the most important leaders in the early church. His story shows that mistakes can help us grow and find new meaning if we ask for forgiveness and make things right.

Making Mistakes and Learning From Them to Get Stronger

The Bible says that the best way to grow spiritually is to

learn from your mistakes. David sinned with Bathsheba and had to deal with bad things happening in his family (2 Samuel 11-12). He truly felt sorry for his actions (Psalm 51), showing that admitting our mistakes can help us understand better and have more faith. Even great leaders make mistakes, but David's story shows that they can come back better after they say sorry.

Job is another great example of someone who suffered a lot and kept their faith. He lost his money, his health, and his family, but he refused to curse God, even though he was in a lot of pain (Job 1:20-22). We can learn a lot about strength from Job's ability to keep going through hard times. He learnt a lot about being faithful and God's power through his experiences.

Keeping Your Faith Through Hard Times

The story of Ruth shows how to keep your faith when things get hard. Ruth stayed with her mother-in-law Naomi after she lost her husband instead of going back to her own family (Ruth 1:16-17). As a sign of her loyalty, she went to work in Boaz's fields, where she finally found favour and got married again. Ruth's dedication shows that staying strong in your faith through hard times can bring you surprising benefits.

During his mission, Paul also went through a lot of hard times, like being jailed, beaten, and having his shipwrecked, but he never lost faith in Christ (2 Corinthians 11:23-28). He wrote a lot about how to be strong when you're weak (2 Corinthians 12:9) and how to depend on God's forgiveness when things get hard.

In short, people in the Bible like Moses, Peter, David, Job, Ruth, and Paul show how to use faith to get through hard times. Their stories show us that sadness can help us grow if we keep trusting God through hard times and learn from our mistakes.

CHAPTER 19:

CONTINUAL GROWTH AND ADAPTATION

- Embracing lifelong learning in your spiritual journey
- Adjusting to new phases of your assignment
- Staying relevant and effective in changing times

Accepting That You Will Learn New Things Throughout Your Life

A lot of people in the Bible showed how to keep learning and growing on their spiritual paths throughout their lives. One important person is King Solomon, who was known for being wise. It is said in 1 Kings 3:5–14 that Solomon asked God for knowledge to lead the people instead of money or a long life. This request shows that he wanted to learn and understand, which was something he did all through his rule. His works in Proverbs and Ecclesiastes show more about his quest for knowledge and understanding, and they stress how important it is to be wise in life.

The Apostle Paul is another example of someone who changed a lot over the course of his life. Paul used to persecute Christians, but his meeting with Christ on the road to Damascus (Acts 9:1–19) was the start of a lifelong process of learning. He spent a lot of time learning the Bible and sharing the Gospel. This is clear from his letters to different churches (for example, Romans 12:2), in which he urges Christians to be changed by having their minds renewed.

Getting Used to The Next Parts of Your Assignment

People in the Bible often had to change their jobs and responsibilities because their situations changed. For example, Moses led the Israelites out of Egypt, but he had to change how he led them while they were wandering in the desert for forty years (Exodus 3-4). At first, Moses wasn't sure about his calling because he felt inadequate (Exodus 3:11). But he learnt how to lead well despite problems through experience.

Esther is another example. She went from being a Jewish girl who had lost her parents to becoming queen of Persia (Esther 2). She showed bravery and flexibility by risking her life to talk to King Xerxes about the problem that was threatening her people (Esther 4:16). Figuring out her new job was very important for keeping her people from being destroyed.

How to Stay Useful and Relevant in Changing Times

Nehemiah's story shows how important it is to be relevant and successful. After hearing that Jerusalem was empty, Nehemiah felt he had to do something (Nehemiah 1). Even though there was resistance, he turned his skills as a cupbearer into leadership as he organised the rebuilding of Jerusalem's walls (Nehemiah 2:17-18). He was able to lead well during a very difficult time because he planned ahead and prayed for help from God.

Similarly, Jesus showed how to be flexible by teaching sailors, tax collectors, and women, among other people. His parables were stories that everyone could relate to and that taught deep lessons that were true for all times and countries (Matthew 13:10-17). Jesus' ability to connect with people from different backgrounds shows that to stay relevant, you need to know your audience and stay true to your goal.

In the end, these examples from the Bible show that accepting that you will learn new things throughout your life, adapting to new stages of tasks, and staying current are all important parts of spiritual growth. We can learn important lessons that we can use in our own lives by looking at these historical figures: Solomon's search for knowledge, Paul's journey of transformation, Moses' flexible leadership, Esther's brave actions, Nehemiah's strategic planning, and Jesus' understandable teachings.

CHAPTER 20:

LIVING YOUR DIVINE PURPOSE DAILY

- Practical steps for daily alignment with your assignment
- Celebrating small victories and progress
- Maintaining joy and gratitude in your journey

Daily Steps to Staying on Track with Your Assignment

To be in daily alignment with your divine purpose, you have to take deliberate actions and keep your mind on completing your calling. Here are some useful steps that are shown with stories from the Bible:

- **Praying and Looking for Direction:** Just like Daniel prayed to find God (Daniel 6:10), people can set aside time every day to pray for guidance and understanding in their lives. This practice helps people stay in line with their goal.

- **Studying the Bible:** Timothy was told to dedicate himself to reading the Bible in public (1 Timothy 4:13). This shows how important it is to spend a lot of time with God's Word to better understand what He wants.

- **Serving Others:** During His time, Jesus showed us how to serve others (Mark 10:45). Serving others, like He did, can help people stay in line with their spiritual purpose because it shows love and dedication to God's goal.

- **Setting Value-Based Goals:** When Nehemiah rebuilt the walls of Jerusalem, he had clear goals in mind (Nehemiah 2:17-18). People can also make personal goals that are in line with their values and spiritual calling. This will help them take steps towards achieving their purpose.

- **Acceptance and Help from the Community:** In Acts 2:42-47, Christians helped and supported each other in the early church, showing the power of community. Joining a group can help you stay motivated and accountable as you follow your special calling.

Celebrate Small wins and Progress

It's important to keep yourself motivated along the way by noticing and enjoying small wins:

- **Recognising Progress:** In Philippians 1:6, Paul says he is sure that God will finish the good work He started in us. Recognising even small successes helps us keep believing that God is working in our lives.

- **Giving Thanks:** The Bible stresses the importance of being thankful all the time. For example, 1 Thessalonians 5:16-18 says to always be joyful and give thanks no matter what. Celebrating small wins helps you keep an upbeat attitude about your journey.

- **Sharing Testimonies:** To celebrate being freed from Egypt, the Israelites told stories (Exodus 15). Sharing your own successes can motivate others and make communities a happier place to live.

- **Setting Up Reminders:** After crossing the Jordan River, Joshua told the Israelites to put up stones as a reminder (Joshua 4:20-24). Making real notes or journals can help people keep track of their progress and celebrate big steps.

How to Keep Your Joy and Gratitude on Your Journey

Being joyful and thankful are important parts of living out your unique purpose:

- **Finding Joy in Service:** In Philippians 4:4, Paul tells us to always be happy. Serving others brings joy and helps you live out your purpose while keeping your mood up.

- **Daily Practice of Gratitude:** Colossians 3:15 says that while we are thankful, we should let peace rule our minds. Practicing thanks every day helps you keep your mind on the good things in life instead of the bad things. When we think about how reliable God is, Psalm 100 tells us to worship him with joy because he is good and trustworthy. When you're going through hard times, remembering the times when God was there for you can help you stay joyful.

- **Encouraging Each Other:** Hebrews 10:24–25 says to encourage each other to love and good works. This helps keep the peace in communities by helping each other on their paths.

These examples from the Bible, can help you successfully align yourself with your holy purpose every day, celebrating your progress and staying joyful along the way.

REFERENCES

- Bible (2018). HOLY BIBLE: KJV.

- Brennfleck, K. and Kay Marie Brennfleck (2005). Live your calling: a practical guide to finding and fulfilling your mission in life. San Francisco: Jossey-Bass.

- Eldredge, J. (2011). Wild at heart—discovering the secret of a man's soul. Thomas Nelson Publishers.

- Henry, M. (2009). Matthew Henry's Commentary on the Whole Bible. Peabody, Mass.: Hendrickson Publishers.

- Murray, A. (1905). Waiting on God. Fig.

- Stanley, C.F. (2008). Understanding Financial Stewardship. Harper Christian Resources.

- Warren, R. (2007). The purpose-driven life : what on earth am I here for, Rick Warren. Zondervan.

- Wiersbe, W.W. (2001). The Bible Exposition Commentary, Volume 1, New Testament. Colorado Springs, Colo.: Victor/Cook Communications.

THE END

www.ingramcontent.com/pod-product-compliance
Lightning Source LLC
Chambersburg PA
CBHW030308100526
44590CB00012B/569